EMMANUEL JOSEPH

Echoes of Evolution, The Neuroscience and Anthropology of Musical Expression

Copyright © 2025 by Emmanuel Joseph

All rights reserved. No part of this publication may be reproduced, stored or transmitted in any form or by any means, electronic, mechanical, photocopying, recording, scanning, or otherwise without written permission from the publisher. It is illegal to copy this book, post it to a website, or distribute it by any other means without permission.

First edition

This book was professionally typeset on Reedsy. Find out more at reedsy.com

Contents

1	Chapter 1: The Birth of Musicality	1
2	Chapter 2: The Rhythms of Life	3
3	Chapter 3: The Power of Melody	5
4	Chapter 4: Harmony and the Human Spirit	7
5	Chapter 5: The Language of Lyrics	9
6	Chapter 6: The Dance of Emotion	11
7	Chapter 7: The Cognitive Symphony	13
8	Chapter 8: The Social Soundscape	14
9	Chapter 9: The Healing Harmonies	15
10	Chapter 10: The Evolution of Musical Instruments	17
11	Chapter 11: The Science of Sound	19
12	Chapter 12: The Future of Musical Expression	21
13	Chapter 13: The Intersection of Music and Technology	23
14	Chapter 14: The Cultural Mosaic of Music	25
15	Chapter 15: The Timelessness of Musical Expression	27

1

Chapter 1: The Birth of Musicality

Paragraph 1: Music, an intricate dance of sound and silence, is an inherent part of the human experience. From ancient drumbeats to the orchestral symphonies of today, our relationship with music has evolved, mirroring the trajectory of human development. The roots of musicality can be traced back to early humans, who used rhythm and melody to communicate, celebrate, and even to survive. It is this primal connection that forms the bedrock of our understanding of music's role in human evolution.

Paragraph 2: Anthropologists have long pondered the origins of music, proposing various theories that highlight its significance in early human societies. One prevailing theory suggests that music emerged as a form of social cohesion, strengthening bonds within groups and facilitating cooperation. The ability to create and respond to music may have conferred evolutionary advantages, enabling early humans to thrive in their environments.

Paragraph 3: Neuroscientists, too, have explored the deep-seated connections between music and the brain. The brain's response to music is multifaceted, involving complex interactions between auditory, emotional, and motor regions. These interactions suggest that music is not merely a cultural artifact but a fundamental aspect of human cognition and emotion. The universality of music across cultures and time periods underscores its importance in the human experience.

Paragraph 4: As we delve into the origins of musicality, it becomes clear that music is more than just a form of entertainment. It is a window into our past, a tool for understanding the development of human society and the intricate workings of the brain. By examining the birth of musicality, we gain insight into the profound impact that music has had on shaping who we are as a species.

2

Chapter 2: The Rhythms of Life

Paragraph 1: Rhythm, the heartbeat of music, is deeply embedded in the human experience. From the steady pulse of our own hearts to the rhythmic patterns found in nature, humans are innately attuned to rhythm. This connection to rhythm is not only biological but also cultural, influencing the ways in which we create and perceive music.

Paragraph 2: In many cultures, rhythm serves as a foundation for musical expression. Drumming, for example, is a universal practice that spans across continents and centuries. The act of drumming taps into our primal instincts, evoking powerful emotional responses and fostering a sense of community. The repetitive nature of rhythm can induce trance-like states, highlighting its potential for altering consciousness.

Paragraph 3: Neuroscientific research has shed light on the brain's remarkable capacity for rhythm perception. The brain's ability to synchronize with external rhythms is crucial for various cognitive and motor functions. This synchronization involves complex neural networks that integrate sensory input with motor output, allowing us to move in time with music and even predict future beats.

Paragraph 4: The rhythms of life extend beyond music, influencing our daily activities and interactions. From walking and talking to dancing and drumming, rhythm plays a central role in how we navigate the world. By exploring the rhythms of life, we gain a deeper appreciation for the ways in which rhythm shapes our experiences and connects us to one another.

3

Chapter 3: The Power of Melody

Paragraph 1: Melody, the soul of music, captivates and enchants listeners with its flowing sequences of notes. It is the element of music that most readily evokes emotion, capable of bringing tears to our eyes or a smile to our faces. The power of melody lies in its ability to tell a story, to convey feelings and experiences in a way that words alone often cannot.

Paragraph 2: Anthropologists have noted the universality of melody, observing that every culture has its own melodic traditions. These melodies are shaped by the natural environment, historical events, and social structures of each society. The universality of melody suggests that humans have an innate capacity to create and appreciate melodic patterns, a capacity that is deeply rooted in our evolutionary history.

Paragraph 3: Neuroscientific studies have explored the brain's response to melody, revealing that melodic processing involves intricate interactions between auditory and emotional regions. The brain's ability to recognize and remember melodies is remarkable, underscoring the importance of melody in our cognitive and emotional lives. The connection between melody and memory is particularly strong, with certain tunes having the power to transport us back to specific moments in our past.

Paragraph 4: The power of melody extends beyond individual experiences, influencing social interactions and cultural expressions. Melodies can serve as cultural symbols, carrying meanings and associations that resonate with entire communities. By examining the power of melody, we gain a deeper understanding of how music connects us to our emotions, our memories, and each other.

4

Chapter 4: Harmony and the Human Spirit

Paragraph 1: Harmony, the blending of different musical notes, is a testament to the beauty of collaboration. In music, harmony enriches melodies and adds depth to compositions. It mirrors the human experience, where cooperation and unity create something greater than the sum of individual parts. The concept of harmony resonates deeply with our social nature and our desire for connection.

Paragraph 2: Anthropologically, harmony can be seen as an extension of social cohesion. In many cultures, singing in harmony is a communal activity that fosters a sense of belonging and shared purpose. The act of creating harmony requires listening and responding to others, highlighting the importance of empathy and cooperation. It is through these harmonious interactions that communities strengthen their bonds.

Paragraph 3: Neuroscientists have studied the brain's response to harmony, finding that it engages both auditory and emotional centers. The pleasure derived from harmonious music is linked to the brain's reward system, which releases dopamine in response to pleasing sounds. This neurological response underscores the profound impact that harmony has on our emotional well-being and our sense of joy.

Paragraph 4: The human spirit thrives on harmony, both in music and in life. By exploring the role of harmony in musical expression, we gain insight into the ways in which collaboration and unity enhance our experiences. Harmony teaches us that working together, whether in creating music or building communities, leads to richer, more fulfilling lives.

5

Chapter 5: The Language of Lyrics

Paragraph 1: Lyrics, the words set to music, add an additional layer of meaning to musical compositions. They transform abstract melodies and harmonies into tangible stories, messages, and emotions. Lyrics have the power to articulate our innermost thoughts and feelings, making them a vital component of musical expression.

Paragraph 2: Anthropologists have studied the role of lyrics in various cultures, noting that they often serve as a means of preserving history, expressing identity, and conveying moral lessons. In many societies, songs with meaningful lyrics are passed down through generations, becoming an integral part of cultural heritage. The ability of lyrics to communicate complex ideas and emotions highlights the significance of language in human evolution.

Paragraph 3: The neuroscience of lyrics is a fascinating field, exploring how the brain processes words set to music. Research has shown that lyrical music engages both language and auditory regions of the brain, creating a unique neural experience. This dual engagement may enhance memory and emotional responses, explaining why certain songs with powerful lyrics leave a lasting impact on listeners.

Paragraph 4: The language of lyrics is a bridge between music and meaning, connecting us to the stories and emotions of others. By examining the interplay between lyrics and music, we gain a deeper appreciation for the ways in which words and melodies combine to create profound expressions of the human experience.

6

Chapter 6: The Dance of Emotion

Paragraph 1: Music has a unique ability to evoke and amplify emotions, creating a powerful connection between the listener and the sounds they hear. This emotional resonance is a testament to the deep-rooted relationship between music and the human brain. The dance of emotion within music is not merely a byproduct of its structure; it is an integral part of the experience.

Paragraph 2: Anthropologists have observed that music often serves as an emotional outlet in various cultures. Whether through joyful celebrations or mournful laments, music provides a means of expressing feelings that might otherwise be difficult to articulate. This emotional expression is not only therapeutic for individuals but also strengthens social bonds by fostering empathy and understanding.

Paragraph 3: Neuroscientists have studied how music affects the brain's emotional centers, such as the amygdala and the limbic system. Music can trigger the release of neurotransmitters like dopamine and serotonin, which are associated with pleasure and mood regulation. This neurological response explains why music can be so profoundly moving and why it plays a crucial role in emotional well-being.

Paragraph 4: The dance of emotion within music is a testament to its power to connect us to our innermost selves and to each other. By exploring the ways in which music evokes and amplifies emotions, we gain a deeper understanding of its significance in our lives. Music is not just a form of entertainment; it is a vital means of emotional expression and connection.

7

Chapter 7: The Cognitive Symphony

Paragraph 1: Music is a cognitive symphony, engaging multiple areas of the brain in a harmonious interplay of auditory, motor, and emotional processes. This complex interaction highlights the cognitive benefits of musical engagement, from enhancing memory and attention to fostering creativity and problem-solving skills.

Paragraph 2: Anthropological studies have shown that musical practices often involve cognitive challenges, such as learning to play an instrument or mastering intricate rhythms. These challenges promote cognitive development and can lead to improved mental faculties. In many cultures, music is an integral part of education, reflecting its importance in cognitive growth.

Paragraph 3: Neuroscientific research has revealed that musical training can lead to structural and functional changes in the brain. For example, musicians often exhibit increased connectivity between brain regions involved in auditory and motor processing. These changes suggest that engaging with music can enhance cognitive abilities and even protect against cognitive decline.

Paragraph 4: The cognitive symphony of music underscores its potential as a powerful tool for mental enrichment. By understanding the cognitive benefits of musical engagement, we can harness its power to improve brain health and foster intellectual growth. Music is not just an art form; it is a means of enhancing our cognitive capacities and enriching our lives.

8

Chapter 8: The Social Soundscape

Paragraph 1: Music is a social soundscape, reflecting and shaping the social dynamics of human societies. It serves as a medium for communication, cultural expression, and social cohesion. The social functions of music are as diverse as the cultures that create it, highlighting its role in fostering community and shared identity.

Paragraph 2: Anthropologists have documented the ways in which music facilitates social interaction, from communal singing and dancing to ceremonial performances. In many cultures, music is a central element of social rituals, reinforcing social bonds and conveying cultural values. The social soundscape of music reveals its power to unite people and strengthen communities.

Paragraph 3: Neuroscientific studies have explored the brain's response to social music-making, such as group singing or playing in an ensemble. These activities engage neural networks involved in social cognition, empathy, and cooperation. The brain's ability to synchronize with others through music underscores its role in promoting social harmony and collective well-being.

Paragraph 4: The social soundscape of music is a testament to its ability to connect us to one another. By examining the social functions of music, we gain insight into how it fosters community and shared identity. Music is not just a personal experience; it is a social phenomenon that brings people together and strengthens the fabric of society.

9

Chapter 9: The Healing Harmonies

Paragraph 1: The healing power of music has been recognized for centuries, with ancient civilizations utilizing melodies and rhythms for therapeutic purposes. Music therapy, a field that continues to grow in prominence, harnesses the restorative properties of music to address various physical, emotional, and cognitive challenges. The healing harmonies of music offer a unique pathway to well-being.

Paragraph 2: Anthropological studies have shown that music is often used in traditional healing practices across cultures. Shamans, healers, and medicine people incorporate music into rituals to promote healing and spiritual growth. These practices highlight the deep connection between music and holistic health, demonstrating that music is more than just an art form—it is a tool for healing.

Paragraph 3: Neuroscientific research has provided insight into the mechanisms behind music's healing effects. Music can reduce stress, alleviate pain, and enhance mood by modulating neural activity in regions associated with emotion and reward. The rhythmic and melodic elements of music can also facilitate motor rehabilitation, making it a valuable therapeutic tool for individuals recovering from neurological conditions.

Paragraph 4: The healing harmonies of music underscore its potential as a powerful adjunct to traditional medical treatments. By understanding the therapeutic benefits of music, we can integrate it into healthcare practices to improve patient outcomes and overall well-being. Music is not just a source of enjoyment; it is a potent healer that can transform lives.

10

Chapter 10: The Evolution of Musical Instruments

Paragraph 1: The evolution of musical instruments mirrors the development of human technology and creativity. From simple percussion instruments to complex orchestral creations, musical instruments have evolved alongside human societies, reflecting cultural advancements and technological innovations. The journey of musical instruments is a testament to human ingenuity and artistic expression.

Paragraph 2: Anthropologists have traced the origins of musical instruments to early human societies, where natural objects like stones and bones were used to create sound. Over time, the development of tools and materials led to the creation of more sophisticated instruments, such as flutes, drums, and stringed instruments. Each culture has contributed to the rich tapestry of musical instruments, adding its own unique innovations and designs.

Paragraph 3: The neuroscience of musical instrument playing reveals the intricate coordination between sensory, motor, and cognitive processes. Learning to play an instrument engages multiple brain regions, promoting neural plasticity and cognitive development. This complex interplay underscores the cognitive benefits of musical training and the profound impact of musical instruments on brain function.

Paragraph 4: The evolution of musical instruments highlights the dynamic relationship between music and human progress. By exploring the history and development of musical instruments, we gain a deeper appreciation for the ways in which music and technology have shaped human culture and cognition. Musical instruments are not just tools for creating sound; they are embodiments of human creativity and innovation.

11

Chapter 11: The Science of Sound

aragraph 1: The science of sound, also known as acoustics, is the foundation of musical expression. Understanding the principles of sound waves, frequency, and resonance is essential for creating and appreciating music. The science of sound bridges the gap between the physical properties of music and its perceptual effects, revealing the underlying mechanisms that make music so captivating.

Paragraph 2: Anthropologists have documented the use of acoustic principles in traditional music-making practices. Indigenous cultures often have a deep understanding of how sound behaves in different environments, using natural acoustics to enhance musical performances. This knowledge reflects the universal human fascination with sound and its potential for artistic expression.

Paragraph 3: Neuroscientists have explored how the brain processes acoustic information, revealing that the auditory system is finely tuned to detect subtle changes in sound. The brain's ability to analyze and interpret complex sound patterns is essential for music perception and appreciation. This intricate processing highlights the sophisticated nature of our auditory system and its role in musical experience.

Paragraph 4: The science of sound provides a deeper understanding of the physical and perceptual aspects of music. By examining the principles of acoustics, we can appreciate the intricate interplay between sound waves and human perception. The science of sound is not just a technical field; it is a gateway to understanding the magic of music and its impact on our lives.

12

Chapter 12: The Future of Musical Expression

Paragraph 1: The future of musical expression is shaped by technological advancements and evolving cultural landscapes. From virtual reality concerts to AI-generated compositions, the possibilities for musical innovation are vast and exciting. The future of music is a dynamic field that promises to transform the way we create, experience, and share music.

Paragraph 2: Anthropologists and ethnomusicologists are exploring how globalization and digital technology are influencing musical traditions. While some fear the loss of cultural diversity, others see opportunities for cross-cultural collaboration and the creation of new musical genres. The future of musical expression will likely be a blend of traditional practices and cutting-edge innovations.

Paragraph 3: Neuroscientists are investigating how emerging technologies can enhance musical engagement and cognitive health. Brain-computer interfaces, for example, hold the potential to allow individuals with disabilities to create and experience music in new ways. These advancements highlight the potential for technology to expand the boundaries of musical expression and accessibility.

Paragraph 4: The future of musical expression is a canvas of endless possibilities. By embracing technological advancements and cultural evolution, we can create new forms of musical art that enrich our lives and connect us across distances and differences. Music is not just a relic of the past; it is a living, evolving force that will continue to shape the human experience for generations to come.

13

Chapter 13: The Intersection of Music and Technology

Paragraph 1: The intersection of music and technology is a vibrant and rapidly evolving field. Technological advancements have revolutionized the way we create, produce, and consume music. From digital audio workstations to streaming platforms, technology has democratized music-making and expanded access to musical content, creating new opportunities for artists and listeners alike.

Paragraph 2: Anthropologists and ethnomusicologists are examining how technology is transforming traditional musical practices. In some cases, digital tools are being integrated into age-old traditions, creating hybrid forms of musical expression. In other instances, technology is enabling the preservation and dissemination of endangered musical cultures, ensuring their survival for future generations.

Paragraph 3: Neuroscientists are exploring how technology can enhance musical experiences and cognitive engagement. Virtual reality (VR) and augmented reality (AR) technologies, for example, offer immersive musical experiences that can engage multiple senses and deepen emotional connections. These innovations highlight the potential for technology to enhance our understanding and appreciation of music.

Paragraph 4: The intersection of music and technology is a testament to human ingenuity and adaptability. By embracing technological advancements, we can push the boundaries of musical expression and create new forms of artistic and cultural experiences. Technology is not just a tool for creating music; it is a catalyst for innovation and transformation in the world of music.

14

Chapter 14: The Cultural Mosaic of Music

Paragraph 1: Music is a cultural mosaic, reflecting the diversity and richness of human societies. Each culture has its own unique musical traditions, shaped by historical events, social structures, and environmental factors. The cultural mosaic of music highlights the interconnectedness of music and identity, as well as the ways in which music serves as a vehicle for cultural expression.

Paragraph 2: Anthropologists have documented the wide variety of musical practices across cultures, from the intricate gamelan orchestras of Indonesia to the vibrant mariachi bands of Mexico. These diverse musical traditions reflect the unique histories and values of each society, highlighting the importance of music as a cultural artifact.

Paragraph 3: Neuroscientists are investigating how cultural factors influence musical perception and cognition. Research has shown that individuals from different cultural backgrounds may perceive and respond to music in distinct ways, shaped by their cultural experiences and musical training. This cultural variability underscores the importance of considering cultural context in the study of music and the brain.

Paragraph 4: The cultural mosaic of music is a celebration of human creativity and diversity. By exploring the rich tapestry of musical traditions, we gain a deeper appreciation for the ways in which music reflects and shapes our cultural identities. Music is not just a universal language; it is a cultural expression that connects us to our histories, our communities, and our shared humanity.

15

Chapter 15: The Timelessness of Musical Expression

Paragraph 1: The timelessness of musical expression is evident in its enduring presence across human history. From ancient civilizations to modern societies, music has been a constant companion, evolving and adapting to reflect the changing times. The timelessness of music speaks to its profound impact on the human experience, transcending temporal and spatial boundaries.

Paragraph 2: Anthropologists have explored the historical continuity of musical practices, noting that many musical traditions have been passed down through generations. These traditions serve as a link between the past and the present, preserving the cultural heritage and collective memory of societies. The timelessness of music highlights its role as a repository of human history and wisdom.

Paragraph 3: Neuroscientists are studying how the brain processes and retains musical information over time. Research has shown that music can evoke vivid memories and emotions, creating a lasting imprint on the brain. This enduring connection between music and memory underscores the timelessness of musical expression and its ability to transcend the limitations of time.

Paragraph 4: The timelessness of musical expression is a testament to its enduring relevance and significance. By understanding the ways in which music has shaped and been shaped by human history, we gain a deeper appreciation for its timeless appeal. Music is not just a fleeting form of entertainment; it is a timeless art form that continues to inspire and connect us across generations.

Echoes of Evolution: The Neuroscience and Anthropology of Musical Expression

"Echoes of Evolution: The Neuroscience and Anthropology of Musical Expression" delves into the profound relationship between music and humanity. This compelling narrative takes readers on a journey through twelve meticulously crafted chapters, each unraveling the intricate dance between our biological, cultural, and cognitive selves as influenced by music.

Starting with the primal beats of our ancestors, the book explores the origins of musicality and how it became an essential part of human communication and survival. It examines the rhythms that shape our daily lives, the melodies that evoke our deepest emotions, and the harmonies that unite us. Through the lens of anthropology, we discover how music serves as a cultural artifact, preserving histories and fostering social cohesion.

Neuroscience reveals the brain's remarkable capacity for musical engagement, from rhythm perception to emotional response, highlighting music's role in cognitive development and emotional well-being. The book also delves into the healing power of music, its cognitive benefits, and the fascinating world of musical instruments and their evolution.

The narrative extends to the modern era, exploring the intersection of music and technology, the cultural mosaic of musical traditions, and the timelessness of musical expression. With each chapter, "Echoes of Evolution" illuminates the multifaceted ways in which music has shaped and continues to shape the human experience.

This thought-provoking exploration offers a deeper understanding of the profound impact of music on our lives, making it an essential read for anyone interested in the enduring connection between music, the brain, and human culture.